GREEN HOPEX

Christian Women with ADHD
Understand and Embrace God's Design for Your Mind

Contents

Preface

Do you ever wonder why everyday life feels like a high-wire act?

One missed step away from chaos? Have you ever stared at another woman's color-coded planner or her seemingly endless patience and thought, "Why can't I just be like that?"

I'm Esther Ellison, and I've spent years believing that if I just tried harder, prayed harder, or pushed through, I could finally catch up. But with ADHD, my reality looked a lot more like forgotten appointments, mountains of laundry, and the deep ache of feeling like I was letting my kids,or my calling down...

Maybe you're a mom, juggling school forms, meal plans, and that never-ending to-do list, and still lying awake at night replaying everything you forgot. Or maybe you're a working woman, feeling like you're always one missed deadline or one lost email away from disaster. Maybe, like me, you walk out of church with a smile but collapse in the car, overwhelmed and wondering if you're missing some spiritual secret everyone else knows.

Sister, you are not broken. You are not less spiritual, less disciplined, or less worthy because your brain works differently. In fact, I believe—deep down—you are fearfully and wonderfully made, even if the world, and sometimes the church, tells you otherwise.

Psalm 139 verse 14 says, "I praise you because I am fearfully and wonderfully made; your works are wonderful, I know that full well." I had to repeat that verse over and over, until it became louder than the lies in my own head.

That's why I wrote Christian Women WITH ADHD. This isn't another self-help book filled with impossible routines or guilt trips. It's my story, and the stories of women just like you… Woven together with Scripture, science, and grace.

Inside, you'll discover the truth about ADHD:

You'll learn why it's not a spiritual weakness or a character flaw. I'll show you practical ways to break free from shame and silence that inner critic that whispers, "You'll never measure up."

Romans 8:1 tells us:
  "Therefore, there is now no condemnation for those who are in Christ Jesus."
  We'll talk about the power of grace-filled routines. Even if you've never finished a planner in your life. How to build real, judgment-free community with other women who actually get it.

You'll find faith-based strategies to pray for clarity, peace, and wisdom on the days your brain feels like a browser with a hundred tabs open. I'll share organization hacks that finally made sense for me, not for some mythical "perfect mom." You'll hear raw stories, my own and others', about forgotten permission slips, burned dinners, and the little victories that matter more than anyone else sees.

And you'll get the "Holy Mess" 3-Minute Morning Routine Guide. A simple, grace-filled way to start your day, even if the rest of your morning goes sideways.

Most of all, I want you to know:

You don't have to wait until you have it all together. "My grace is sufficient for you, for my power is made perfect in weakness."

God tells us in 2 Corinthians 12 verse 9. You don't need perfect focus or superhuman willpower to experience God's peace and joy. You are already loved, already enough, right here, right now.

If you're tired of feeling behind, ashamed, or invisible. If you're longing for a faith community that celebrates your quirks and encourages your gifts. This book is for you. You'll find hope, practical help, and the gentle reminder that you're not alone.

With this book I wanted you to understand yourself better. This book is the foundation of the next book.

"Christian Women with ADHD: The 7-Steps to Overcome Distractions, Declutter, and Flourish in Relationships & Finances Based on God's Word"

we will dive into more practical daily tips and discover more about Adhd and *you*.

Scan the upcoming QR code to get many more practical tips and dive deeper into how to use your hidden talents.

https://amzn.to/4meKYnZ

So let's begin.

Because the truth is, God doesn't make mistakes...

And you, sister, are His masterpiece.

Bonus

Struggling to start your day with peace instead of chaos?
Want to reset your mornings and embrace God's peace daily?

The **Holy Mess 3-Minute Morning Reset** is a simple, grace-filled tool to
help you ground your ADHD mind quickly and intentionally.

Download your free 3-Minute Morning Reset here →

Start small. Start with grace.

(Instant access when you sign up for encouragement and updates!)

One

Letter from the Heart: To the Woman Who's Tired of Hiding

❧

"I praise you, for I am fearfully and wonderfully made."
—Psalm 139:14

"Therefore, there is now no condemnation for those who are in Christ Jesus." —Romans 8:1

"My grace is sufficient for you, for my power is made perfect in weakness." —2 Corinthians 12:9

Dear Sister,

Maybe no one else sees it, but you do—the silent weight you carry every day. The feeling that your life is a jumble of reminders, lost keys, interrupted prayers, and half-finished lists. You're the first to volunteer at church, the last to leave the group text unread, and somehow still the one who feels like she's "too much" and "not enough" all at once.

I know what it's like to pour yourself into everyone else's needs, only to lie awake at night with that ache of "Why can't I just get it together?" Maybe you try to hide the messy parts—the piles, the forgotten dates, the time you lost your train of thought mid-sentence in small group and felt the sting of embarrassment for hours afterward. Maybe you hold back from sharing, from shining, from really being seen—because somewhere along the way, you learned that "different" meant "defective."

But let me tell you the truth:

You are not broken. You are beloved.

You are not a problem for God to solve. You are His masterpiece—fearfully and wonderfully made, knit together with infinite detail, including the wild, beautiful, dazzling way your mind works.

Even the parts that trip you up, the parts you wish you could exchange for something "easier"—God looks at those and calls you good.

Scripture is clear: there is no condemnation in Christ Jesus. That shame you feel? That's not your portion. God's power is made perfect not in your performance, but in your weakness. His love runs deeper than every "oops" and "I'm sorry" and "maybe next time." He meets you in the mess—not with a finger of accusation, but with open arms of grace.

I wrote this letter because I needed it myself, once. I needed someone to tell me I wasn't lazy, or crazy, or failing. I needed to know that being "wired differently" didn't disqualify me from God's love, purpose, or joy. If you're here, maybe you need that too.

You are not too much. You are not behind.

You are not invisible to God.

You are not broken. You are beloved.

So, let's do this together. Let's lay down the masks and the hiding places. Let's bring our full, unfiltered selves into the light of God's love, and see what happens when we stop striving to be "normal" and start living as the women He created us to be.

Because, friend, you are wanted here. You belong—in all your beautiful complexity.

Welcome. I'm so glad you're here.

With love,

Esther

A Note from the Authors

Welcome, dear reader.

We are honored to walk alongside you on this journey. Whether you are newly diagnosed, have known about your ADHD for years, or simply suspect your mind works a little differently, we want you to know: this space is for you.

This book is not a clinical manual, and it's not just a list of tips and tricks. It's a conversation—a companion for the real-life, beautiful, complicated path of women with ADHD who are also women of faith. We know the courage it takes to even open these pages. You may be holding years of silent struggle, stories of being misunderstood, or hopes that "maybe this time will be different." Take a breath. You're in good company.

We want to be clear:

ADHD is not a spiritual failing or a character flaw. It's a brain-based difference that brings its own set of challenges *and* gifts. Our hope is that as you read, you'll find not just information, but *validation*. You'll see yourself in these stories and realize you are not alone—and you never have been.

We invite you to bring your whole self—your doubts, your hopes, your faith, your questions. Along the way, we'll weave together research, practical tools, honest stories, and, above all, the unshakable promise of God's grace. Because we believe that grace is not just a theological idea, but a daily reality you can lean on.

So, as you begin this book, may you feel welcomed, seen, and blessed. We pray that you will come to know, deep in your bones, that God's love for you is not dependent on your performance, productivity, or perfection. His grace is enough—for every moment, every mess, every step of this journey.

Enjoy the ride. You are beloved.

With love and gratitude

Two

Part 1: YOU ARE NOT BROKEN — YOU ARE BELOVED

❧

Welcome to the Sisterhood

"I praise you because I am fearfully and wonderfully made; your works are wonderful, I know that full well." — *Psalm 139:14*

Ever feel like you're the only one whose brain runs on its own chaotic frequency? Have you ever hidden the real you, worried that your brand of "different" is just too much—or not enough?

If you're reading this, you've probably spent years trying to fit into a mold that just wasn't made for you. Maybe you've prayed for self-control, for order, for focus—hoping God might trade in your scattered thoughts for something tidier. Maybe you've left church events with a smile, only to collapse in the car feeling like an imposter, convinced you're missing the "normal" gene everyone else seemed to get at birth.

Sister, exhale. You are not an accident. You are not broken, defective, or lazy. You are beautifully wired—handcrafted by a God who delights in every part of you.

This is the beginning of a different kind of journey. You're not joining a club for the "damaged" or a support group for women who need fixing. You're joining a sisterhood—a community of women who are finally ready to drop the shame, peel off the mask, and step into the truth: **God doesn't make mistakes, and you are fully seen and fully loved.**

What You'll Discover in This Chapter

- Why you've felt like an outsider for so long (and why that's not your fault)
- How difference is not a curse, but a calling
- The first, radical step to embracing your beautifully-wired self
- A gentle reframe: You are not a problem to be solved

The Myth of "Normal"

In our Christian circles, there's this unspoken standard—"the good woman." She's organized, reliable, hospitable. Her purse holds tissues, mints, and the secret to a clutter-free home. She's on time, she remembers birthdays, and her prayer journal is always up to date.

But let's be real: most of us are juggling grocery lists, carpool, and the swirl of unfinished tasks in our heads. When you add ADHD to the mix, it's easy to feel like you're living in a different universe, watching other women with awe—or envy.

The world, and often the church, holds up "normal" as the goal. But what if there is no standard brain? What if neurodiversity—brain difference—is as God-designed as the variety of flowers in a garden?

Thomas Armstrong, a champion of neurodiversity, puts it this way: "Instead of pretending there's a perfectly 'normal' brain to which all others must be compared, we need to admit there is no standard brain... diversity among brains is just as wonderfully enriching as biodiversity." That's not just psychology; that's holy creativity.

You Are Not Alone—You Are Better Together

The enemy loves to isolate. Shame says, "You're the only one who can't keep it together." But here's the truth: countless women—brilliant, loving, Jesus-following women—share your struggle. You are part of a community of extraordinary, kindred companions walking this ADHD journey.

It takes real courage to show up as you are, to drop the act, and to let yourself be known. Especially when your differences are invisible to everyone else—except you.

For years, I felt like I had to hide the mess to be accepted. I compared my behind-the-scenes chaos to everyone else's highlight reel. But God, in His kindness, led me to others who understood. Women who let me be real, who celebrated my wins—tiny and huge—and didn't flinch when I missed the mark.

We were never meant to do this alone. **Your struggles do not disqualify you from community—they are often the doorway in.**

Stop Waiting to Be Fixed

Let's address the "fix me" myth head on. Maybe you've wondered how many therapy sessions it'll take before you finally get your act together. Or you've prayed for the quick miracle—the instant download of self-discipline.

But here's the hard and beautiful truth: you are not a problem to be solved. You are not a project in need of repair. Only furniture need fixing! God is not waiting for you to get organized before He uses you.

What if the goal isn't to become "normal," but to become **whole**? What if your quirks, your energy, your passion, your way of seeing the world—what if these are gifts meant to be embraced, not erased?

"My grace is sufficient for you, for my power is made perfect in weakness." — 2 Corinthians 12:9

Sister, it's not about becoming someone else. It's about becoming more of who God made you to be.

Reflection: Your Beautifully Wired Self

- What messages did you hear growing up about being "different"?
- In what ways have you tried to hide or "fix" yourself?
- What might it look like to accept, even delight in, the unique wiring God gave you?

Two Practical Steps

- **Find Your People:** Reach out to one trusted friend or online group where you can share something real—no filter. Notice how it feels to be honest, even in a small way.
- **Affirm the Truth:** Write Psalm 139:14 somewhere you'll see it daily. When the inner critic pipes up, say it out loud: "I am fearfully and wonderfully made."

Find others on the same journey

Want to find your people? You're invited to join our private Facebook group— a safe, grace-filled space just for Christian women navigating ADHD. Inside, you'll meet sisters who "get it"—who understand both your struggles and your faith, and are eager to offer support, laughter, and real-life tips. You don't have to walk this path alone; community is waiting, and your story belongs here.

Blessed Christian Women: ADHD Support Community of Faith

https://www.facebook.com/groups/blessedchristian-women

How ADHD Works (and Why You Feel Like You're Failing)

Scripture Spotlight

"Therefore, there is now no condemnation for those who are in Christ Jesus."
— *Romans 8:1*

Have you ever wondered, "Why can't I just get it together?" Or felt the weight of "should"—as in, "I should be able to do this"?

If you have ADHD, you're likely familiar with the sinking sense that you're always just a step behind. Appointments missed, keys misplaced (again), conversations where you zone out halfway through. It can feel like there's an invisible wall between you and the life you're "supposed" to be living.

But what if the reason isn't laziness, carelessness, or lack of faith? What if it's simply your brain's wiring?

What's Actually Going On in Your Brain

Here's the short version: ADHD isn't a "deficit" of attention—it's a challenge with *regulating* attention, emotions, and actions. Your brain is beautifully different, with unique patterns in how it manages focus, memory, motivation, and even how you feel things.

Think of your brain like a symphony orchestra—each musician (memory, focus, organization, emotion) is talented. But sometimes, the conductor—the part that coordinates everything—misses a cue. The result? Beautiful music, but sometimes a little chaotic.

ADHD affects what science calls "executive function"—the brain's management system. This can make it tough to:

- Start and finish tasks (even ones you *want* to do)
- Stay organized (hello, piles of laundry)
- Manage time (wait, it's already 3:00?)
- Remember details (like the password you just set…yesterday)
- Regulate emotions (big feelings, fast and fierce)

This is not your fault. These are symptoms—not your soul.

The Lie of "Try Harder"

If you've heard "Just focus!" or "You'd remember if it mattered," you're not alone. The world sees the missed deadlines, the scattered papers, the forgotten birthdays. But few see the invisible marathon you run just to show up every day.

ADHD is not a character flaw. It is not a failure of willpower or faith. It's a brain-based, lifelong difference that can make everyday tasks exhausting. And yet—because your differences are mostly invisible—others (and maybe you) have mistaken symptoms for laziness or lack of effort.

Let's set the record straight:

- You are not lazy.
- You are not stupid.
- You are not broken.

You're living with a brain that plays by different rules.

Grace Over Guilt

Jesus did not come to pile on more "shoulds." He came to set you free. Romans 8:1 promises: "There is now no condemnation for those who are in Christ Jesus." That includes you, right now, messy brain and all.

Where others see a problem, God sees a person. Where you see failure, He sees a beloved daughter who keeps showing up.

Reflection: Releasing Condemnation

- Where have you been confusing symptoms for sin?
- What would it look like to approach your challenges with grace instead of guilt?

Two Practical Steps

1. **Name the Symptom:** The next time you forget, fidget, or space out, pause and say, "That's my brain, not my worth." Practice separating the symptom from your identity.
2. **Micro-Compassion:** When you catch yourself slipping into "I'm so…" (lazy, dumb, messy), stop and reframe. Try, "This is hard for me—and I'm still loved."

The Inner Critic vs. the Voice of God

Scripture Spotlight

"Therefore, do not conform to the pattern of this world, but be transformed by the renewing of your mind." — *Romans 12:2*

Ever notice how loud your inner critic can be? That voice that says, "You're not enough. You'll never get it together. Why even try?"

For women with ADHD, the soundtrack of self-doubt often plays on repeat. It's not just the missed deadlines or the lost keys—it's the *story* you tell yourself about what those moments mean. Shame sneaks in, whispering that you're less than, always one step behind, never quite measuring up.

But friend, those voices are not from God.

The Source of the Inner Critic

Most of us didn't invent our inner critic from scratch. It's stitched together from years of messages—some direct, some implied:

- Teachers who sighed, "If you'd just apply yourself..."
- Family who joked about your forgetfulness
- Church friends who didn't understand why you couldn't just "be more disciplined"

Layer by layer, we absorb these beliefs until the critic sounds just like our own thoughts. But here's the truth: your inner critic is often just an echo of old shame, not the voice of your Savior.

Romans 8:1 declares, "There is now no condemnation for those who are in Christ Jesus." Full stop.

God's Voice Sounds Different

God's voice doesn't shame, belittle, or accuse. The enemy is called the "accuser of the brethren" for a reason (Revelation 12:10). Jesus' words bring conviction, not condemnation; hope, not humiliation.

If you've internalized the lie that your struggles make you less lovable or less Christian, it's time to untangle that knot. The renewing of your mind (Romans 12:2) isn't about fixing yourself—it's about replacing lies with truth.

You are not the sum of your struggles. You are God's handiwork, created in Christ Jesus for good works (Ephesians 2:10).

A New Narrative: Trading Shame for Truth

Let's be honest: learning to recognize the inner critic takes practice. But the more you name it, the less power it holds. The next time you hear, "You'll never get it right," try asking: "Is this what God says about me?"

Spoiler: God says you're chosen, loved, and called. He is not waiting for you to meet some invisible standard before He delights in you.

A Story of Unlearning

I once coached a woman named Laura who, after decades of masking her ADHD, received a diagnosis in her forties. "I'm a hot mess," she confessed in our first meeting, laughing but also half-apologizing for her entire self. She could recite her failures by heart—but when asked about her strengths, she drew a blank.

Slowly, Laura began to notice the critic's voice. She'd pause, breathe, and ask, "Whose voice is that?" With practice, she swapped self-criticism for curiosity. Over time, she learned to let God's truth drown out the static. Her confidence grew—not because the struggles vanished, but because the shame lost its grip.

Reflection: Whose Voice Am I Listening To?

- What is one lie your inner critic has told you this week?
- What does God's Word actually say about you in that area?
- Imagine speaking to yourself with the same compassion you offer a friend—what would change?

Two Practical Steps

1. **Scripture Swap:** Write down one negative self-belief and tape a countering Scripture beside it (Romans 8:1, Romans 12:2, Psalm 139:14). Read it aloud each morning.
2. **Practice Pause:** When the inner critic shouts, pause and ask, "Is this true? Is this kind? Is this what Jesus would say to His daughter?" If not, release it.

Reflective Takeaway: You Are Not Broken—You Are Beloved

If you've spent years believing you're too much, not enough, or somehow defective, let this truth sink deep: **God does not make mistakes. He made you on purpose, for a purpose—even with your beautifully unique brain.**

ADHD is not your identity. It's not your fault. It's not a spiritual failure. It's one part of your story—a story God is weaving with more grace, more love, and more possibility than you can imagine.

In this sisterhood, shame loses its power. You can bring your whole self—

14

messy, scattered, passionate, creative—to the table. You are not broken. You are beloved.

Summary of Practical Steps

1. Find Your People: Share your honest story with someone safe.

2. Affirm Your Worth: Speak Psalm 139:14 over yourself daily.

3. Name the Symptom, Not blaming the Soul: Remember, these are brain differences, not character flaws.

4. Swap Critic for Christ: Challenge negative self-talk with Scripture.

5. Pause and Pray: When shame flares, ask God to remind you of who you really are.

If you're ready to drop the weight of shame and walk in belovedness, you're in the right place dear. This is just the beginning.

Three

Part 2: Untangling the Lies You've Believed

❧

"You will know the truth, and the truth will set you free."
— **John 8:32**

A Strong Start: The Lies That Shape Us

Let's get real: Most of the time, the battle for joy and confidence isn't fought with planners or productivity hacks—it's fought in your mind, in the quiet places no one else sees.

Have you ever noticed that some of your deepest pain doesn't come from "having ADHD," but from what you (and others) have *decided* that means? The "shoulds," the shame, the years of absorbing silent messages like, "Why can't you be more like her?" or "Good Christian women always have it together."

The result? You start wearing those words as labels—broken, lazy, too much, not enough. You try harder, shrink smaller, play safe. The lies get so tangled into your story that you forget they ever had an author.

But here's the radical truth: **Jesus didn't die and rise so you could live by lies. He came to set captives free—including from the invisible cages of**

shame.

This part of your journey is about seeing the lies for what they are, letting go, and learning to listen to the voice of Truth—the One who made you.

What You'll Learn In This Section

- How shame grows from old messages, not your real worth.
- Why hiding is our go-to survival move (and how to gently stop).
- The cost of playing small, and the freedom of stepping into your God-given light.
- How to start replacing shame with scripture and support.
- Two practical steps to break free, today.

Chapter 1: The Messages That Shaped Your Shame

Who Told You That You Were Broken?

Pause. Close your eyes. When did you first feel "different"? Maybe it was the first time you forgot your homework, or when you spaced out during Sunday school and someone noticed. Maybe you just always felt "out of sync," like the world was an inside joke you missed the punchline to.

For me, it was a hundred small moments—teachers sighing, friends rolling eyes, well-meaning adults saying "try harder." By the time I got my ADHD diagnosis, the inner critic had already taken up permanent residence.

Let's name the four main sources of shame messages:

1. **You Messages:** The blunt comments—"You're lazy." "You're so scattered." "What's wrong with you?"
2. **She Messages:** The whispered judgments about others—"Her house is

a disaster." "She can never remember anything."

3. **Duh! Messages:** The well-meaning "fixes"—"Just use a planner." "Set a timer!" "Everyone forgets sometimes."

4. **Absorbed Messages:** The unspoken cultural scripts—"A good Christian woman is always organized, serene, and sacrificial. She never asks for help."

Which ones shaped you most?

For me, it was all of them. The You Messages made me shrink. The She Messages made me pretend. The Duh! Messages made me feel stupid and unheard. The Absorbed Messages? Those dug deepest—because I never even noticed I was carrying them.

Scripture for the Battle

"For God has not given us a spirit of fear, but of power and of love and of a sound mind."

— 2 Timothy 1:7

Notice that: power, love, sound mind. No mention of "perfection," "people-pleasing," or "never missing a deadline."

Story: Clarissa's Family Table

Clarissa always felt out of place at her big Cuban family gatherings. She loved her culture, the laughter, the chaos. But every time someone pointed out her "spacey" ways or asked why she wasn't married yet, a wave of shame crashed over her. She tried harder—bringing dishes to potlucks, arriving early to help, stuffing her mouth with empanadas so she wouldn't blurt out the wrong thing. But inside, she felt like she was failing the very people she loved.

It wasn't until Clarissa started meeting with a trusted cousin—someone who saw beneath the surface—that she realized those messages weren't the truth of who she was. They were just stories, passed down, fueled by love and fear and tradition. The real truth? Clarissa's unique brain was part of her calling. Her family didn't need her to be a clone—they needed her to be herself.

Reflection: What Did You Hear?

- What was "difference" called in your house growing up? Was it creative, quirky, or just "too much"?
- Who made the rules about what women "should" be like?
- How did church, school, or community reinforce those rules?

Write down three old "messages" you're ready to question.

Your quick feedback is my blessing:

If this book has encouraged you or helped you feel less alone, would you leave a quick review?

Even one sentence makes a huge difference and takes just a minute. As a small author, your feedback not only lifts my heart—it also helps other women of faith with ADHD find the support and hope they need.

Thank you for being part of this journey!

https://www.amazon.com/review/create-review?asin=1956493263

Chapter 2: The Hiding Game (And the Cost of Playing Small)

Why Do We Hide?

Let's call it out: Christian women with ADHD become experts at hiding. Sometimes it's conscious—we "pass for normal," never invite people over, pretend to laugh at jokes about "flaky" women. Sometimes it's invisible—we apologize for existing, say yes when we want to scream no, avoid volunteering or leadership roles because "what if they see the real me?"

Why do we do it?

Because the pain of being misunderstood, judged, or rejected feels unbearable. Because we've learned—rightly or wrongly—that being "different" is dangerous.

But here's the secret: **Hiding keeps us safe for a while, but it also keeps us small.**

Eden's Story: Who Told You To Hide?

Remember the Garden of Eden? Adam and Eve eat the fruit, realize their nakedness, and hide. God's first question is not, "What have you done?" It's, "Where are you?" and "Who told you that you were naked?" (Genesis 3:9, 11).

God isn't asking because He's lost track of His kids. He's asking because He wants them to see: shame is a thief, not a friend.

What are the "fig leaves" you use to hide? Over-apologizing? Overcommitting? Staying silent instead of speaking truth? For me, it was all of the above.

The Cost of Hiding

It's easy to think hiding is harmless, but it actually extracts a steep price. You miss out on:

- Opportunities to lead, serve, or shine.
- Deeper connections with friends and family.
- Using your God-given strengths in the church and the world.

- Real intimacy—with God, others, and yourself.

In trying to protect ourselves from pain, disappointment and disconnection, we often wall ourselves off from the very joy we crave.

Story: Irene's Girls' Trip

Every year, Irene's sisters and cousins planned a "girls' weekend." In theory, it sounded fun—sisterhood, laughter, a break from daily life. In reality, Irene dreaded it. She worried she'd forget something important, get overwhelmed by the noise, or be labeled "high-maintenance" for needing quiet time.

So Irene hid her discomfort, suffered in silence, and came home exhausted and resentful. She longed for connection, but her shame kept her stuck.

Sister, what "trips" are you avoiding? What gatherings, projects, or callings are you sitting out—not because you're unqualified, but because you're afraid to be seen?

Reflection: What's the Price of Hiding?

- What relationships, opportunities, or dreams have you skipped because you were afraid of being "found out"?
- How does hiding make you feel: safe, or more alone?

List one area where hiding is costing you more than it's helping.

Chapter 3: Why Playing Small Hurts Your Soul

The Rules We Never Questioned

Somewhere along the way, most of us learned the "rules" of womanhood—rules that are sometimes louder in the church than anywhere else.

- Don't make waves.
- Be nice, agreeable, and accommodating.
- Don't ask for special treatment, even if you need it.
- Don't stand out, don't outshine, don't be "too much."

Sound familiar? The problem is, for women with ADHD, these rules are a minefield. Our brains literally won't let us fit. Trying harder doesn't fix it; it just makes us feel like failures.

And so, we shrink. We play small. We let shame tell us, "Stay quiet. Don't risk it. Don't let them see."

Scripture: You Are Called to Freedom

"For freedom Christ has set us free; stand firm therefore, and do not submit again to a yoke of slavery."
— Galatians 5:1

You were not called to a life of silent suffering. Jesus died to set you free—not just from sin, but from the shackles of "never enough."

Deb's Story: The Odd Mom Out

Deb lived in a shiny suburb where the women were always put together, the houses always sparkling, the schedules always full. Every holiday, she felt her anxiety and shame ramp up. She loved her family, but the pressure to host, bake, and keep up the old traditions was suffocating.

Deb kept quiet, didn't ask for help, and felt like a failure every December. But deep down, she longed for the courage to say, "Can we do things differently this year?"

What about you? Are there roles or rituals you feel trapped by? Who made the rule that you have to do it all, perfectly, without help?

Reflection: Whose Expectations Are You Serving?

- Are you living to please God—or to avoid disappointing people?
- Where are you following "tradition" that doesn't serve your soul (or your family)?

Write down one tradition, expectation, or role you want to reevaluate.

Chapter 4: The Voice of Truth

Replacing Lies With God's Voice

Here's the best news: Just because you've believed a lie for years doesn't mean you have to carry it one more day.

The world says: "You're too much."

God says: "You are wonderfully made." (Psalm 139:14)

The world says: "You'll never change."

God says: "I am doing a new thing!" (Isaiah 43:19)

The world says: "Don't stand out."

God says: "Let your light shine before others." (Matthew 5:16)

Practical Takeaway: Make a Shame vs. Truth Chart

Grab a piece of paper and draw two columns:

- **Lie / Shame Message**
- **God's Truth**

For example:

Lie / Shame

God's Truth

I'm too disorganized

God is not a God of confusion but of peace (1 Cor. 14:33). He made me for peace.

I am a burden

"Come to Me, all who are weary…" (Matt 11:28) — I am invited, not a bother.

I must do it all

"My grace is sufficient for you" (2 Cor. 12:9). I can ask for help.

I don't belong

"Now you are the body of Christ, and each one of you is a part of it." (1 Cor. 12:27)

Read your "truth column" out loud every morning this week.

Breaking the Hiding Habit

This is not about becoming loud, pushy, or drawing attention to yourself for attention's sake. It's about becoming visible—to yourself, to God, and to the world. Jesus called His followers the "light of the world," not the "wallflowers of the world."

It might feel risky. The critic will whisper, "You're not ready. You'll just fail again." But you get to choose which voice you believe.

Story: Alexis's Leap

Alexis always dreamed of running her own business. She finally saved up, made a plan, and got ready to launch. But when it came time to tell her friends and family, all her old fears came roaring back: "Who do you think you are? You're just going to prove everyone right—that you're impulsive, emotional, too much."

But Alexis didn't back down. She named her fear, prayed through it, and chose to trust the truth: God made her for a purpose. She took the leap, found support, and discovered her new "scary" dream was exactly what God had prepared her for.

Reflection: Where Are You Being Called to Step Out?

- Is there a conversation you've been avoiding, a talent you've been hiding, a prayer you're scared to pray?
- What's one "small brave" you can try this week—telling a friend the truth, asking for help, saying "no" when you mean it?

Write it down. Pray for courage.

Chapter 5: How to Begin Untangling

Practical Step 1: Name Your Shame

Shame thrives in silence. The first way to fight back is to name it out loud.
Tell a safe friend, a therapist, or just journal: "I feel ashamed when _____. I'm
afraid people will think _____."

Shame is like mold—it dies in the light.

Practical Step 2: Find Your People

You are not meant to do this alone. Jesus chose disciples. Paul had friends
and partners in every city. Even Moses needed Aaron to hold up his arms.

Find or build a small circle—maybe just one person—who gets it, who
can remind you of grace when you forget. Bonus points if they also have
a "different" brain. There is healing in shared laughter, and comfort in not
having to explain every detail.

Scripture for the Road

*"Therefore encourage one another and build each other up, just as in fact you are
doing."*
    — 1 Thessalonians 5:11

A Word About Professional Help

Sometimes, untangling the deepest lies requires a wise counselor, coach, or spiritual director. That's not weakness—it's wisdom. God delights when we pursue healing, in any form.

Ending Reflection: God's Truth Sets You Free

The process of untangling isn't a one-and-done deal. Lies creep back. Old habits return, especially under stress or exhaustion. But every day, every moment, you can choose to come out of hiding, to drop a little more shame, to listen for the Voice that calls you "beloved."

Remember, the Good Shepherd leaves the 99 to find the one who's hiding. He's not annoyed. He's delighted to bring you back into the light.

Takeaways & Practical Tips

1. Make a Shame vs. Truth Chart.

Every time you catch yourself believing a lie, add it to the chart and write God's answer.

2. Practice one "small brave" each day.

This could be as simple as saying "no" when you mean it, asking for help, or sharing your real story with a safe friend.

3. Speak God's truth over yourself.

Pick a verse from this chapter and say it out loud every morning—especially on the messy, doubting days.

4. Reach out for support.

If you don't have a "tribe," ask God for one. It could be a Christian women's group, an online ADHD community, or even just one honest friend.

Final Reflection: Your True Name

When you strip away all the messages—what's left? Daughter. Beloved. Chosen. Redeemed. "See what great love the Father has lavished on us, that we should be called children of God!" (1 John 3:1)

The enemy wants you tangled up in shame. Jesus wants you free. You are not too much, not too messy, not too late. You are enough—because He is enough.

So let's untangle, together.

Four

Part 3: A New Kind of Brave: Radical Acceptance and the Doorway of Grace

❦

"But he said to me, 'My grace is sufficient for you, for my power is made perfect in weakness.' Therefore I will boast all the more gladly about my weaknesses, so that Christ's power may rest on me."
—2 Corinthians 12:9

Have you ever stood in front of your bathroom mirror, toothbrush dangling from your hand, and asked God, "Is it possible to make peace with the mess in my mind?" Maybe you've whispered it during a women's Bible study, or while staring at a planner whose pages are empty except for half-finished lists and reminders you never checked off.

If you have ADHD, you already know the exhaustion of trying to be "better," "together," or "just like everyone else." Maybe you've prayed for God to fix your forgetfulness, begged Him to take away the distractions, or promised yourself that *this time* you'll get it right. And yet... here you are. Still you. Still wired just a bit differently than everyone expects. And maybe, just maybe, still hoping there's a way to love yourself as God loves you—even when you feel tangled inside.

Sister, welcome. You're exactly where you need to be.

In this chapter, you'll discover:

- Why radical acceptance is not resignation, but a brave act of grace.
- How science and Scripture both speak to our wholeness, even when we feel "broken."
- Practical steps to walk in daily acceptance—without giving up on growth.
- Two actionable tips for cultivating this new kind of brave.

Let's open the door together. Let's find out what it means to live loved, messy and all.

The Wound of "Never Enough" — Why Acceptance Feels Radical

Let's be honest: The word "acceptance" can trigger all kinds of feelings. For Christian women, it might sound dangerously close to "giving up." Haven't we been taught to "press on" (Philippians 3:14), to be transformed, to aim for the Proverbs 31 woman who rises before dawn and keeps her home in order? But for those of us with ADHD, that standard is not just hard—it can be a daily source of shame.

What does radical acceptance look like for a Christian woman with ADHD? It's not letting go of hope or growth. It's letting go of the myth that you have to earn your worth by getting it all right.

Why Science Agrees: You're Wired for Difference, Not Deficiency

ADHD is not a character flaw. It's a brain-based difference—affecting how you regulate focus, energy, time, emotion, and yes, sometimes even your mouth at the worst moments. Research shows ADHD is tied to unique patterns in the brain's executive functioning system. These are not "excuses." They're explanations.

But here's the problem: When you don't understand your brain, you start believing the lie that *you* are the problem. Every missed appointment, every impulsive comment, every lost bill becomes evidence that you're broken, lazy, or too much.

Sister, hear this: **You are not a problem to be solved. You are a person to be loved—by God, by others, and by yourself.**

Grace, Not Perfection

God's grace is not a participation trophy for the perfect. It is the power that meets us exactly where we're weakest. When Paul writes, "My power is made perfect in weakness" (2 Corinthians 12:9), he's not talking about some distant, theoretical struggle. He's talking about the kind of persistent, daily difficulty that never fully goes away. The thorn in your flesh. The inbox you never quite clear. The child whose schedule you forgot, again.

God isn't waiting for you to "fix" your brain so He can use you. He's waiting for you to let Him be strong in the very places you feel weakest.

The Myth of Self-Fixing: Only Dogs and Furniture Need Repair

The world loves a fixer-upper story. We want a "before and after"—preferably with a pretty photo and a tidy ending. But the truth is, radical acceptance is messier. It's not a single moment. It's a journey, a "yes" to living in grace every day, even as you keep growing.

Science Echoes Scripture

Therapists who work with ADHD have a saying: "You cannot shame yourself into progress." Research confirms that self-criticism actually worsens executive functioning, increases anxiety, and saps the very motivation you need to grow. In other words, the more you beat yourself up, the harder it becomes to get unstuck.

But here's what's beautiful—when you replace self-condemnation with self-compassion, your brain actually works *better*. You are more resilient, more creative, more able to bounce back from mistakes. Science proves what Scripture's been whispering all along: **Love—real, unconditional love—is** the soil where growth happens.

Acceptance Is Not Resignation

Maybe you fear that accepting your ADHD means giving up. Here's what radical acceptance *really* means:

- Letting go of the lie that "if I just tried harder, I'd be normal."
- Honoring your actual needs, not some impossible standard.
- Choosing to live in reality, not wishful thinking.
- Believing that God's grace is enough, even when you (and your to-do list) are not.

Acceptance is the foundation, not the finish line. It's the platform on which you can build a life that works *for you*, not just for everyone else.

Story: Paula's New Peace

Let's meet Paula—a real woman (with some details changed) who struggled for years to accept her ADHD. Paula was a loving mom and a gifted writer, but she lived in a constant state of overwhelm. Bills stacked up, birthday cards went unwritten, and her car was a "disaster zone," as she put it.

For years, Paula prayed for God to "fix her," but the breakthroughs came not when everything changed, but when her *perspective* did. She realized that even with medication and strategies, there were always going to be piles, missed appointments, and days when her mind just felt scattered.

Instead of hating herself for it, she chose to focus on her strengths. She poured her energy into her blog, encouraging other women. She started to see her struggles as part of her testimony—not a shame to hide, but a story to share. The mess didn't magically vanish, but her sense of worth did. She began to believe that she was loved—messy car and all.

Her takeaway? "God isn't asking me to have it all together. He's asking me to let Him love me right here, in the middle of it."

Radical Acceptance: Living in Grace, Not Perfection

What Is Radical Acceptance?

Let's get practical. Tara Brach, a renowned psychologist, calls radical acceptance "the willingness to experience ourselves and our life as it is." For the Christian, this means seeing yourself through God's eyes—beloved, chosen, and purposeful—even when you don't measure up to the world's standards.

It's not about giving up on growth. It's about giving up on shame.

Why Is It So Hard?

Radical acceptance feels radical because every message in our culture (and often, our churches) tells us to "try harder," "do more," and "fix yourself." Sometimes even the messages from childhood—"You just need to apply yourself"—linger in the background, making us believe that acceptance equals laziness, resignation, or settling.

But in God's Kingdom, *grace* is the foundation for transformation, not its reward. Isaiah 43:1 reminds us: "Do not fear, for I have redeemed you; I have summoned you by name; you are mine." God knew exactly what He was getting when He called you His own. There is nothing about your wiring that surprises Him.

How to Practice Radical Acceptance (Daily Grace, Not Once-and-Done)

1. Name Reality—Gently

The first step is to acknowledge, without judgment, what is true. "I am forgetful. I am creative. I lose things. I make people laugh. I get overwhelmed easily. I care deeply. I am loved." Try writing a list of truths about yourself—both the struggles and the strengths.

2. Separate Symptoms from Soul

ADHD is a set of symptoms. It is *not* your character. If you burned the dinner, lost your wallet, or missed a deadline, that is a behavior, not your identity. Scripture says, "There is now no condemnation for those who are in Christ Jesus" (Romans 8:1). Condemnation is the enemy's language—not God's.

3. Give Yourself Permission to Be Human

Sometimes the bravest thing you can do is simply to be kind to yourself. When you mess up, imagine how you would speak to a friend. Practice saying those words to yourself: "It's okay. You're doing your best. You are still loved."

4. Ask God to Fill the Gaps

You will have gaps. Every woman does. Instead of hustling to hide them, ask God to fill them with His strength. Make this a simple, daily prayer: "Lord, let Your power be made perfect in my weakness. I give You my cracks—shine through them."

Scripture Weaved In

Throughout the Bible, we see a God who chooses the unexpected. Moses, slow of speech. Peter, impulsive and often distracted. Martha, busy and overwhelmed. Yet God did not disqualify them—He used them, right in the middle of their messes.

Paul pleaded three times for his "thorn in the flesh" to be taken away, but God answered, "My grace is sufficient for you" (2 Corinthians 12:9). Grace is not a reward for finally getting it right; it's the gift that holds you when you're not even close.

Isaiah 43:1 is your anchor: "Do not fear, for I have redeemed you; I have called you by name; you are mine." You belong. Not because you've mastered your mind, but because your Maker delights in you.

Reflection: Where Do You Need Grace?

Take a quiet moment. Close your eyes and breathe deeply. Ask yourself:

- Where am I still striving for perfection instead of accepting grace?
- What is one thing about my ADHD that I find hardest to accept?
- What would it look like to offer myself kindness in that area, today?

Jot your answers in a journal. Pray over them. Invite God's gentle voice to speak louder than your inner critic.

Takeaway: You Are Already Enough

Here's the truth the enemy wants you to forget: **You do not have to be "fixed" to be fruitful.** God can and will use you, right now, right here, in all your glorious imperfection. The journey of radical acceptance is not about giving up on growth—it's about choosing grace as the soil for all your becoming.

The bravest women are not the ones who appear flawless, but the ones who allow themselves to be fully seen and fully loved—by God, by others, and by themselves.

2 Practical Tips for Radical Acceptance

1. The "Grace Statement" Habit

Pick one sentence you can whisper to yourself when the old shame stories rise up. For example:

- "This is hard, but I am still God's beloved."
- "I am allowed to be a work in progress."

• "God's grace covers me."

Write it on a sticky note. Put it in your planner or on your bathroom mirror. Let it interrupt the old scripts.

2. Practice "Compassionate Pausing"

When you catch yourself spiraling—after a mistake, a forgotten detail, or a rough day—pause. Literally, put your hand on your heart, breathe deeply, and pray: "Jesus, help me see myself as You do—messy, loved, chosen."

Closing Blessing

Sister, you are not your mistakes, your mess, or your mind's chaos. You are not too much or too little. You are beloved. Christ's power is shining through your very weaknesses—turning every crack into a channel for His light.

May you walk bravely in the freedom of grace. May you accept the beautiful, complicated, dazzling woman God made you to be. And may you discover, day by day, that radical acceptance is the bravest, most faith-filled thing you can do.

Reflection Questions

1. What are three things about your ADHD that you find hard to accept?
2. Where do you most need to receive God's grace in your daily life?
3. How can you remind yourself, practically, of your belovedness this week?

Final Thoughts

Radical acceptance doesn't mean you stop growing. It means you finally have permission to grow from a place of love—not fear. It's the door God longs for you to walk through. Will you step into it?

Scripture references: 2 Corinthians 12:9, Isaiah 43:1, Romans 8:1, Philippians 3:14

Your actionable steps:

- Choose and use a grace statement every day this week.
- When you catch yourself in self-criticism, practice a compassionate pause and invite God's loving perspective.

Let this be the week you choose a new kind of brave. Let this be the week you say: "God's grace is enough—for even me."

Five

You've Come So Far... and There's More Ahead

P ause for a moment and look back at where you started. Maybe when you first picked up this guide, you were running on empty—hoping for relief, but secretly bracing for disappointment. Maybe you felt alone in your struggles, or certain that your "mess" disqualified you from the life you hoped for.

But now? You've named your shame. You've learned to spot the lies you've carried—and you've heard a new voice, speaking truth and grace over your life. You've opened the door to radical acceptance, and you're learning that you are not broken, but beloved.

This is a big deal. You are not who you were at the beginning of this journey.

But can I be honest? There is still so much more ahead. You're not meant to settle here—not when God has even greater freedom, clarity, and confidence waiting for you. None of us "arrives" this side of heaven, but every step you take matters. As you keep moving forward, you'll keep untangling old patterns, growing in your identity, and building a life that feels both possible *and* purposeful.

And here's the best news: you don't have to do it alone.

We're working on a more in depth version of this book—a stronger companion for your faith, your wiring, and your dreams. More stories, more practical tools, more spiritual nourishment. And we can't wait to share it with you.

Your quick feedback is my blessing:

If this book has encouraged you or helped you feel less alone, would you leave a quick review?

Even one sentence makes a huge difference and takes just a minute. As a small author, your feedback not only lifts my heart, it also helps other women of faith with ADHD find the support and hope they need.

Thank you for being part of this journey!

https://www.amazon.com/review/create-review?asin=1956493263

Next Steps: Want to Go Deeper?

If these pages have stirred something in you—a flicker of hope, a new sense of belonging, or simply a hunger for more—you're not alone. God's not done writing your story, and neither are we.

The in-depth version of this book is HERE!

Here's what's coming soon, just for you:

- Guided prayer and devotionals, rooted in Scripture and practical for real life
- Deeper identity work to help you untangle from shame and live boldly as God's beloved
- Spiritual tools and values-based life planning to help you thrive with your unique wiring
- Reflection prompts, action steps, and encouragement for the journey ahead
- Plus: an audiobook version you can listen to on the go—perfect for busy, beautifully-wired women!

"Christian Women with ADHD: The 7-Steps to Overcome Distractions, Declutter, and Flourish in Relationships & Finances Based on God's Word" by Esther Ellison

Scan the QR code below to get your copy now! If it does not work, search for the title on Amazon <3

https://amzn.to/4meKYnZ

Reflection Tools:

Shame vs. Truth Chart

Want a quick way to shut down shame? Swap it for biblical truth.

Sometimes the lies are so familiar, we don't even notice them. That's why I created this simple side-by-side chart—a cheat sheet for your heart, when old stories try to take over. Here's a sneak peek:

Shame Lie
God's Truth

"I'm too much."

God made me with purpose. (Psalm 139:14)

"I'll never get it together."

His grace is sufficient. (2 Cor. 12:9)

"I'm lazy."

I am His workmanship. (Eph. 2:10)

"No one understands me."

God sees and knows me. (Psalm 139:1-3)

"I'm not enough."

I am loved—right now. (Romans 8:1)

"I should hide my struggles."

God's power is made perfect in weakness.

Want to print the full chart?

Download your "Shame vs. Truth" Chart here →

(Free instant access when you sign up for encouragement and the chance to be one of the first people to get our next book for free)

To get the chart above, you can use the same QR code below.

Struggling to start your day with peace instead of chaos?
Want to reset your mornings and embrace God's peace daily?

The **Holy Mess 3-Minute Morning Reset** is a simple, grace-filled tool to
help you ground your ADHD mind quickly and intentionally.

Download your free 3-Minute Morning Reset here →
Start small. Start with grace.
(Instant access when you sign up for encouragement and updates!)

Want to be the first to know when it's available?

Join our email community for early access to my next books, more free tools, and encouragement you can actually use. (No spam, just the good stuff.)

Let's keep going, together.

Click here to get all your bonuses AND updates on the next books →

https://greenhopex.com/Grace-Opt-in

Find others on the same journey

Want to find your people? You're invited to join our private Facebook group—a safe, grace-filled space just for Christian women navigating ADHD. Inside, you'll meet sisters who "get it"—who understand both your struggles and your faith, and are eager to offer support, laughter, and real-life tips. You don't have to walk this path alone; community is waiting, and your story belongs here.

Blessed Christian Women: ADHD Support Community of Faith
https://www.facebook.com/groups/blessedchristianwomen

Sister, your journey is just beginning.

Let's walk this path of grace, truth, and wholehearted living—side by side.

www.ingramcontent.com/pod-product-compliance
Lightning Source LLC
Chambersburg PA
CBHW070031030426
42335CB00017B/2381